Usborne
Little First Stickers
Diwali

Illustrated by Kamala Nair

With expert advice from Sreya Rao

Designed by Yasmin Faulkner
Edited by Holly Bathie

Getting ready for Diwali

Diwali is the Indian festival of lights. Families decorate their houses, dress up in their best clothes and celebrate together with lots of food and gifts. This family is going to have a Diwali celebration tonight.

Stick on all the bright clothes they will wear at the party later.

Painting rangoli patterns

At Diwali, people draw or paint bright rangoli patterns on the ground near the entrance of their homes. Add stickers to help finish the children's patterns.

Lighting diyas

Diyas are small clay lamps that people light as part of a traditional Diwali. Stick on everything Supraja and Sravya need to decorate diyas, ready for the festival of lights.

Use the stickers to decorate
these diyas, then stick on little
tealights to make them glow.

Decorating the house

It's time to put up decorations for the celebration. Add hanging paper lanterns, and bright diyas to the scene.

Baking sweet treats

People give gifts of sweets at Diwali. Stick on the family making all different kinds to give to their friends.

Add all the stickers and labels for these traditional Diwali treats.

barfi

ladoo

nankhatai

kaju katli

phenori

ghughra

Celebrating Diwali

Now everyone is dressed up and ready to celebrate together. Stick on the family and friends sharing food and giving each other gifts.

Enjoying fireworks

The festival of lights wouldn't
be complete without fireworks
lighting up the sky. Fill the
scene with brilliant bangs
and fantastic flashes.

Special Diwali

There are so many things that make Diwali celebrations special. Can you remember them all? Stick some on here.

kurta

sari

anarkali

dupatta

accessories

barfi

nankhatai

phenori

rangoli pattern

diya

lanterns

sweets

dupatta

sari

kurta